To:

From:

Les Environs de Quebec,
France avec Titre d'Evêché; Situés sur la R[a]
Minutes de Longitude, et a 46 degrez 55

IROQUOIS MER DES IROQUOIS

Sorel ent

NOUV. ANGLETERRE

Georges
Wells
Excester
Norfolke
Pescatoro
Salisbury
Charles Down

Nouv. York
Gerland
Albanie
Dierfield
Northampton
Ipswiche
Cambrige
Salem
Boston
Dorcester
N. Bristol

Nouveau Jerfey
Espee
Harford
Wallefton
Milford

Penfylvanie
Conoçoo
Sasquahanneq
Balemore
Philadelfie
Neu Cas tel
Dorin ton
Andas toques
Elisabeth
Bradkinton
Perth
Ambroy
Amboy
Bedford
Oxford
I. Longue
Southampton
de la Pete

Nouvelle Mariiande
Claver ton
Brit tol
Elizabeth
Henry
James ton
Montakin

de Deleware
Summerset
I. de Smith
I. de Smith
Cap Henry
Etats

R. DE VIRGINIE DE LA NOUV

I. Pakeck
I. Raonack
Cap Hetteras

ERD

Passport to the Soul

A Lifelong Journey

Compiled by Beth Mende Conny

Photographs by Beth Ludwig-Khalfayan

PETER PAUPER PRESS, INC.
WHITE PLAINS, NEW YORK

For Deb,
a fellow traveler

Photographs copyright © 2001
Beth Ludwig-Khalfayan/
Wild Apple Licensing

Text copyright © 2001
Peter Pauper Press, Inc.
202 Mamaroneck Avenue
White Plains, NY 10601
ISBN 0-88088-517-3
Printed in China
14

Visit us at:
www.peterpauper.com

Passport to the Soul

A Lifelong Journey

Introduction

Passport to the Soul

is a gentle journey to lands undiscovered yet intimately familiar. Step by step, page by page, you'll learn more about yourself—your Higher Self— and ways to embrace and celebrate life.

Each lovingly chosen quote is a vista, allowing you to see beyond the peaks and valleys of everyday life and into your heart of hearts, for it is there that your true dreams lie.

So dream on! Journey on! Let this passport to your soul be your ticket to the stars.

—B. M. C.

Wherever you

are is the

entry point.

KABIR

It is good to have an
end to journey towards;
but it is the journey that
matters in the end.

URSULA K. LE GUIN

We never know how

high we are

Till we are called

to rise.

EMILY DICKINSON

The real voyage of
discovery consists
not in seeking new
landscapes, but in
having new eyes.

MARCEL PROUST

[B]less not only the road but the bumps on the road. They are all part of the higher journey.

JULIA CAMERON

Chance is always powerful.
Let your hook be
always cast; in the pool
where you least expect it,
there will be a fish.

OVID

Dreams are . . .
illustrations from
the book your soul is
writing about you.

MARSHA NORMAN

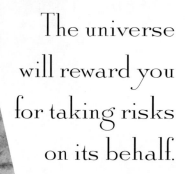

The universe
will reward you
for taking risks
on its behalf.

SHAKTI GAWAIN

To love and be loved
is to feel the sun
from both sides.

DAVID VISCOTT

Follow your instincts.
That's where true
wisdom manifests itself.

OPRAH WINFREY

To be tested is good.
The challenged life may
be the best therapist.

GAIL SHEEHY

I have found that
if you love life,
life will love you back.

ARTHUR RUBINSTEIN

There is only
one journey.
Going inside yourself.

RAINER MARIA RILKE

The mystical journey
drives us into ourselves,
to a sacred flame at
our center.

MARIANNE WILLIAMSON

The road is smooth.
Why do you throw
rocks before you?

ANCIENT EXPRESSION

Our body and our minds
can take us only so far:
Our Spirit can lead us
all the way Home.

SUSAN JEFFERS

One opens the inner
doors of one's heart to
the infinite silences of the
Spirit, out of whose abysses
love wells up without fail
and gives itself to all.

THOMAS MERTON

We are each spinning
our individual threads,
lending texture, color,
pattern, to the "big design"
that is serving us all.

KAREN CASEY

Direct your eye right inward,
and you'll find
A thousand regions
in your mind
Yet undiscovered.
Travel them and be
Expert in home-cosmography.

HENRY DAVID THOREAU

The Promised Land always lies on the other side of the wilderness.

HAVELOCK ELLIS

The life we want is
not merely the one we
have chosen and made.
It is the one we must be
choosing and making.

WENDELL BERRY

Your diamonds are not
in far distant mountains or in
yonder seas; they are
in your own backyard,
if you but dig for them.

RUSSELL H. CONWELL

Take the gentle path.

GEORGE HERBERT

You have to leave the city of your comfort and go into the wilderness of your intuition. What you'll discover will be wonderful. What you'll discover will be yourself.

ALAN ALDA

The great thing in
this world is not so
much where we stand,
as in what direction
we are moving.

OLIVER WENDELL HOLMES

When you come to
a fork in the road,
take it.

YOGI BERRA

The quieter you become,

the more you can hear.

RAM DASS

Look at yourself
through your soul's eyes.
See the beauty of
your being.

SANAYA ROMAN

We need a path,
not to go from
here to there,
but to go from
here to here.

JAKUSHO KWONG

The wind and the waves are always on the side of the ablest navigators.

EDWARD GIBBON

He who would learn
to fly one day must first
learn to stand and walk
and run and climb and
dance; one cannot
fly into flying.

FRIEDRICH NIETZSCHE

No problem can
be solved from the same
consciousness that
created it. We must learn
to see the world anew.

ALBERT EINSTEIN

It's where we go,
and what we do when
we get there, that tells
us who we are.

JOYCE CAROL OATES

If I could know me,
I could know
the universe.

SHIRLEY MacLAINE

We are not human
beings trying to
be spiritual.
We are spiritual beings
trying to be human.

JACQUELYN SMALL

The purpose of
life is to increase
the warm heart.

DALAI LAMA

What you are is
God's gift to you;
what you make
of yourself is your
gift to God.

GEORGE WASHINGTON CARVER

[A]nyone in a state of
seeking can never be happy.
Only those who are constantly
finding are fulfilled.
And finding is not something
that happens to us—
it is something we *do*.

ALAN COHEN

If you do not change
direction, you may
end up where you
are heading.

LAO-TZU

Whatever you want, wants you!

MARK VICTOR HANSEN

When the future becomes far more interesting than the present, the destination holds more importance than the journey.

THOMAS J. LEONARD
WITH BYRON LAURSEN

The aim of life is to live,
and to live means to be aware,
joyously, drunkenly,
serenely, divinely aware.

HENRY MILLER

The privilege of a
lifetime is being
who you are.

JOSEPH CAMPBELL

A knowledge of
the path cannot be
substituted for putting
one foot in front of
the other.

M. C. RICHARDS

[C]hoice is a divine teacher, for when we choose we learn that nothing is ever put in our path without a reason.

IYANLA VANZANT

The reality of time
exists only within us.

CHIN-NING CHU

Take your hands off
the steering wheel.
Be able to say to
the Universe,
"Thy will be done."

GARY ZUKAV

There are no mistakes,
no coincidences.
All events are
blessings given to
us to learn from.

ELISABETH KÜBLER-ROSS

And when you have

reached the mountain

top, then you shall

begin to climb.

KAHLIL GIBRAN

Know your limits,
not so that you can honor
them, but so that you can
smash them to pieces and
reach for magnificence.

CHÉRIE CARTER-SCOTT

Life is a gift, and it offers
us the privilege, opportunity,
and responsibility to give
something back by
becoming more.

TONY ROBBINS

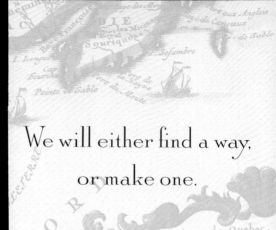

We will either find a way,

or make one.

HANNIBAL

Anyone can carry his burden, however hard, until nightfall. Anyone can do his work, however hard, for one day. Anyone can live sweetly, patiently, lovingly, purely, till the sun goes down. And this is all that life really means.

ROBERT LOUIS STEVENSON

[A]n open mind is
like an open window.
It lets the fresh air in.

MIKE HERNACKI

The curious paradox
is that when I accept
myself just as I am,
then I can change.

CARL ROGERS

Like all explorers,

we are drawn to discover

what's waiting out there

without knowing yet

if we have the courage

to face it.

PEMA CHÖDRÖN

Until you know that
life is interesting—
and find it so—
you haven't
found your soul.

GEOFFREY FISHER

People often say that this or that person has not yet found himself. But the self is not something that one finds. It is something that one creates.

THOMAS SZASZ

To abolish all valleys
is to get rid of all
mountains.

ALAN W. WATTS

It is the soul's duty to be
loyal to its own desires.
It must abandon itself
to its master passion.

REBECCA WEST

Every flower is
a soul blossoming
in nature.

GÉRARD DE NERVAL

The assistance you need will be provided by the universe as soon as you convert your readiness to willingness.

WAYNE W. DYER

We must not cease from exploration. And the end of all our exploring will be to arrive where we began and to know the place for the first time.

T. S. ELIOT

[O]nly you can
discover your gifts
because only you
know what you love.

BARBARA SHER

There's only one
corner of the universe
you can be certain of
improving and that's
your own self.

ALDOUS HUXLEY

CAP

BAYE FRANÇOISE

DIE

Baye des Mines

Fort aux Anglois

Fort les Micmacs

Baye de Camceaux

Royal

SOURIQUOIS

de Sable

I. Longue

P. Sesambre

Cap Fourchue

Port de la Haye

Port du Moute

Pointe de Sable

NORD

TERRE

NEUVE

NORD

Les Environs de Quebec,

France avec Titre d'Evêché, Située sur la R.

Minutes de Longitude, et a 46 degrez 55

la Canardiere

Port Passage

IROQUOIS Mr. Chambly

DES

MOHAWK GEOFF...

Iroque Sorel NOUV. ANGLETERRE Georges

Chute Excester Wells

Nouv. York Dierfield Norfolke Bedeck

Corland Northampton Ipswiche Salisbury

Albanie Windsor Cambrige Charles Down

Esope Hartford Saleme

Andastegues Hulleton Boston

Mitford Dorcester

Conogoge Elisabeth Dr. Bristi

Sasquahanoug Bridinston T.

Philadelp Perth Amboy de Ra

Neu Cas Amboy de N...

Dorin Santley I. Longue

ton Southampton

de Delaware I. de Cats

Summerset de Smith

Clave Henry de Smith

James Cap Henry

Monakin

Nus R.

la Lacague I. Pakeck

I. Raonack

Cap Hetteras

Dokhout

NOUVEAU JERSEY

Pensilvanie

Mrilande

Virginie

RIVIERE DE VIRGINIE DE LA NOUV

MER D